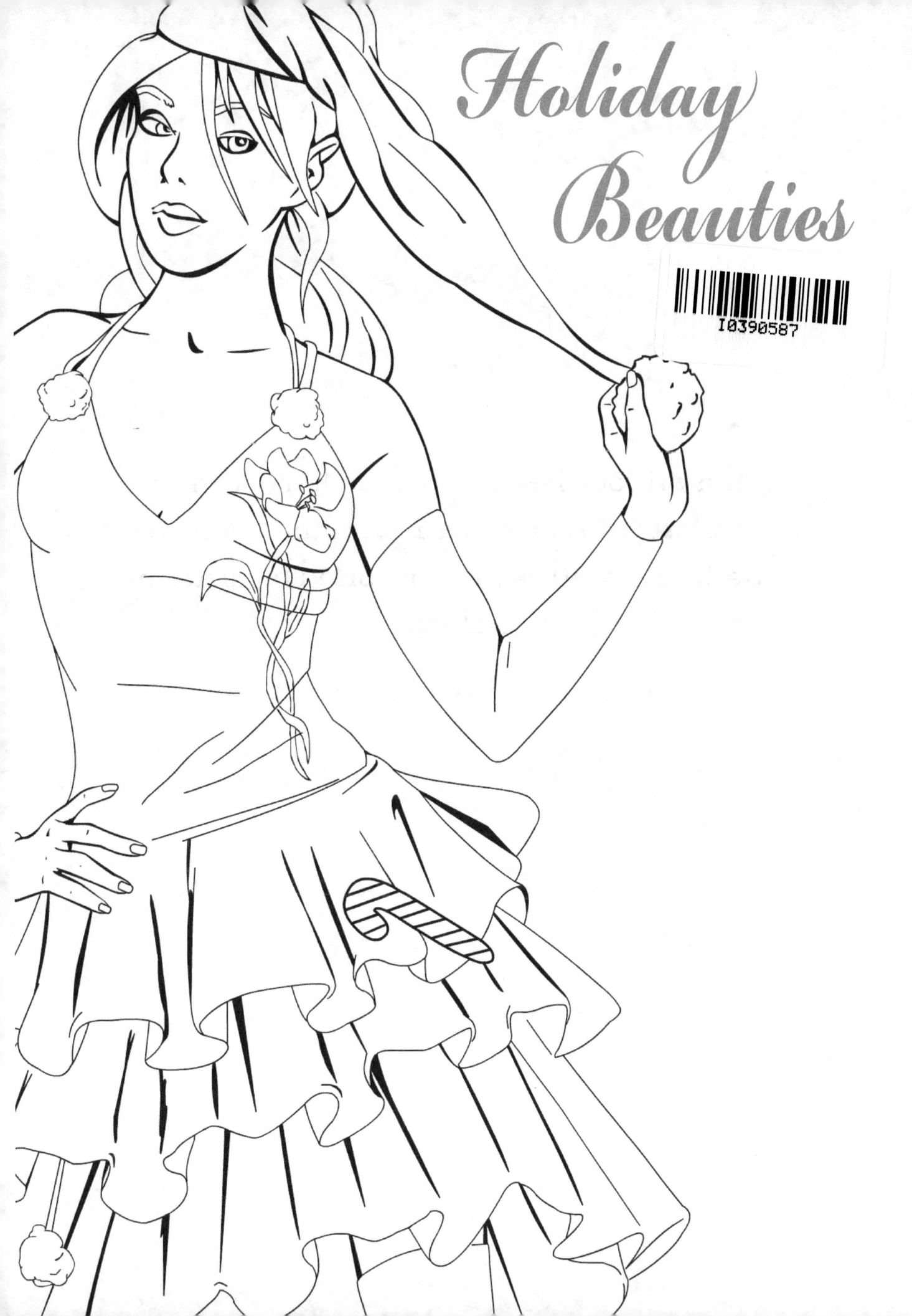

Holiday

Beauties

This artbook features twenty hand-drawn illustrations showcasing original dress designs as well as styles inspired by modern fashions.

Thank you for buying this third edition of Fashion Sketchbook series; a coloring book collection of hand-drawn illustrations by Stephen A Parks.

Discover the full collection:
• Elven Beauties
• Beach Beauties
• Holiday Beauties
• Gothic Beauties {Fall 2017}

Dedications
Thank you Jennifer for helping with the outlines.

Roxie Manello models a candy cane swirl dress and feather hat combo featured in a vintage Coca-Cola ad.

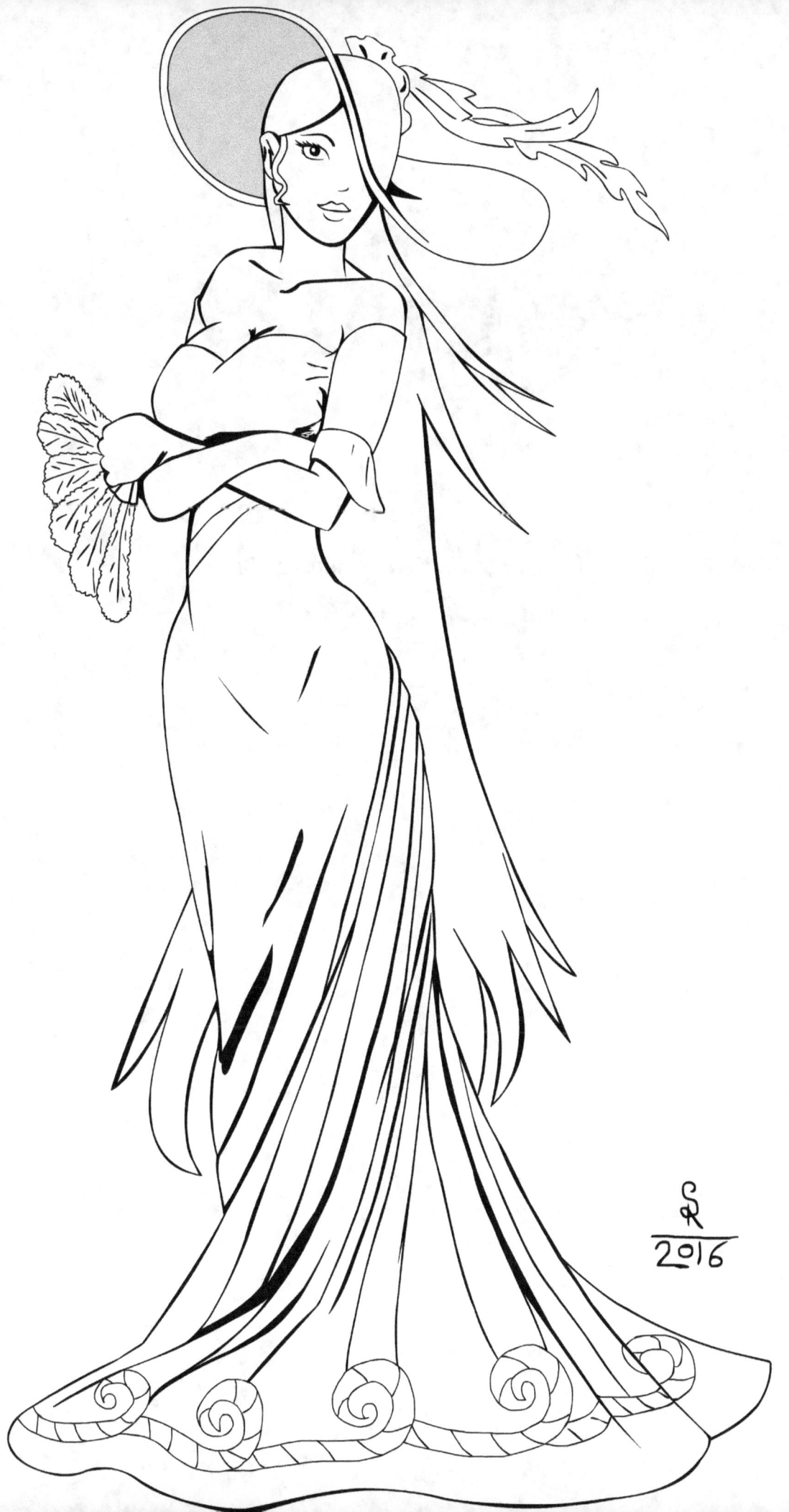

Ava Dubrow Menorah Dress

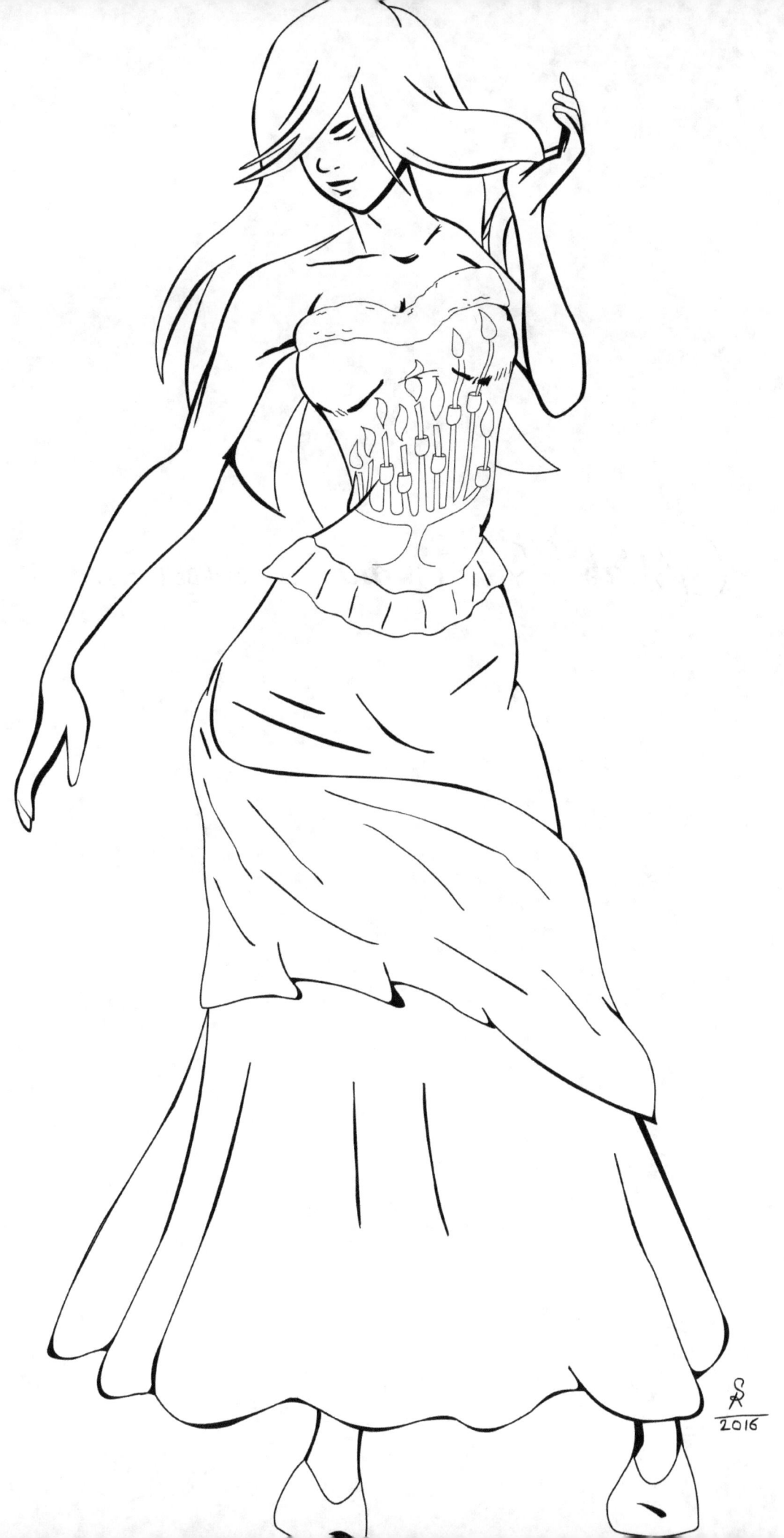

Mabel Swann Bow-and-Bell dress

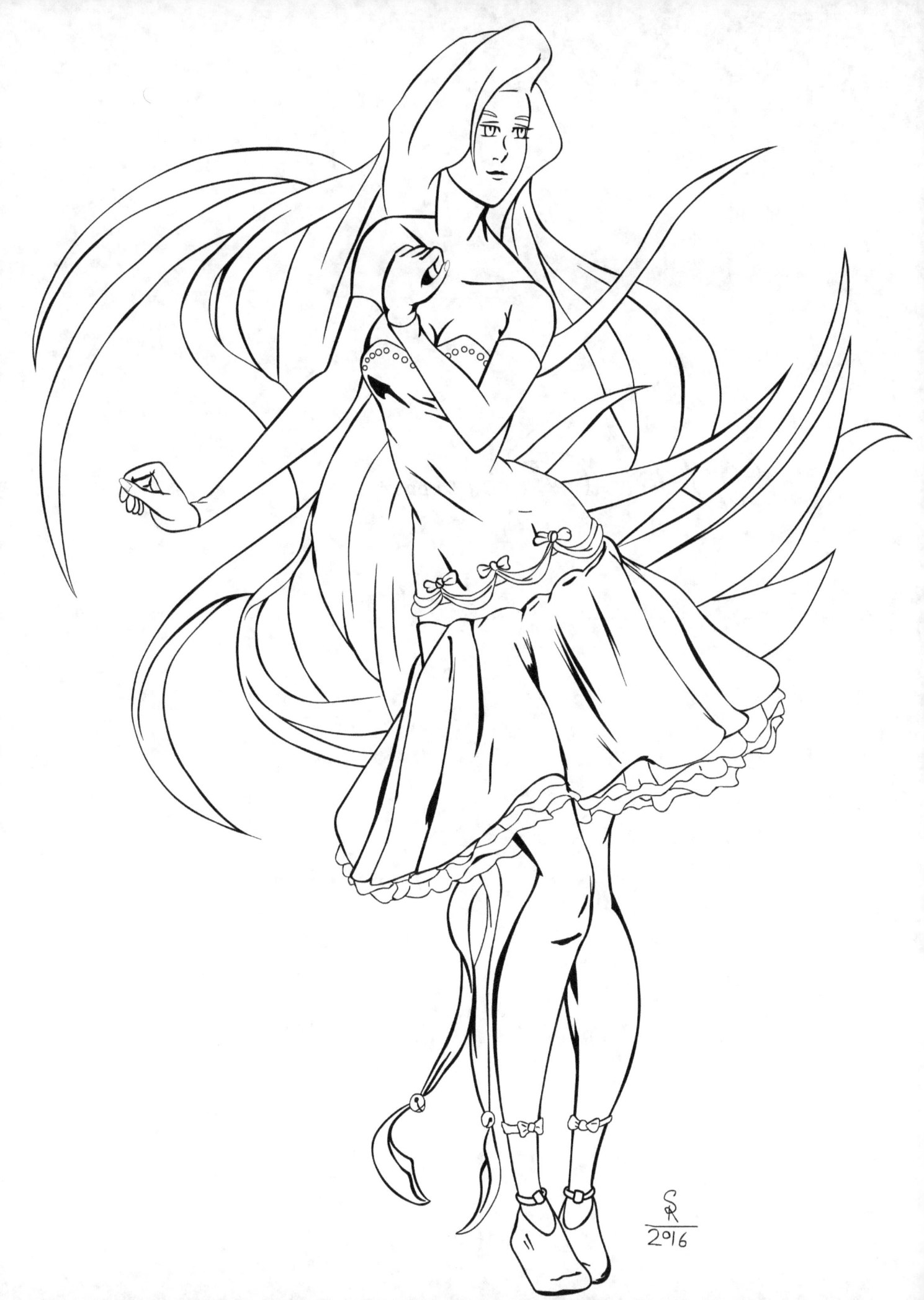

Chelsea Tate Surprises

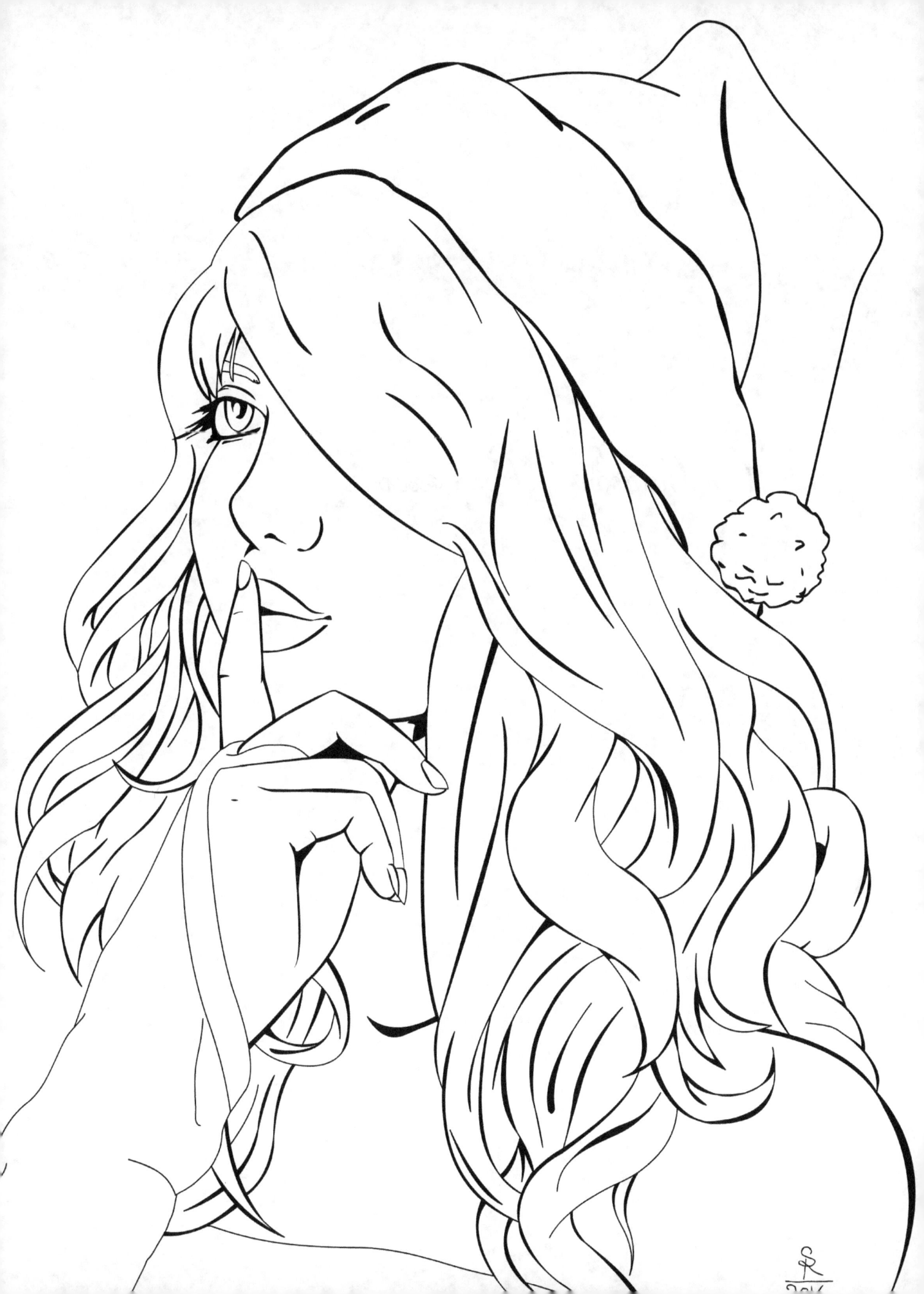

Madison Poe Yesod Dress

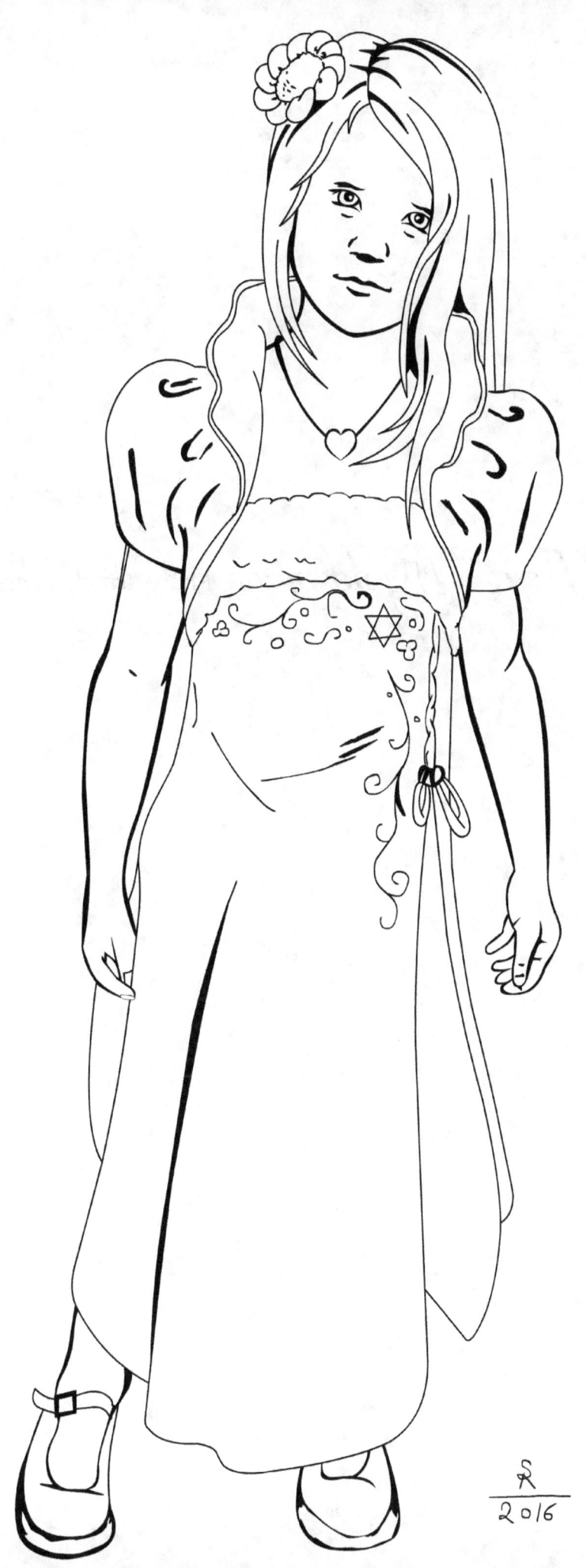

Tessa Goldwynn Krissy Kringle Dress

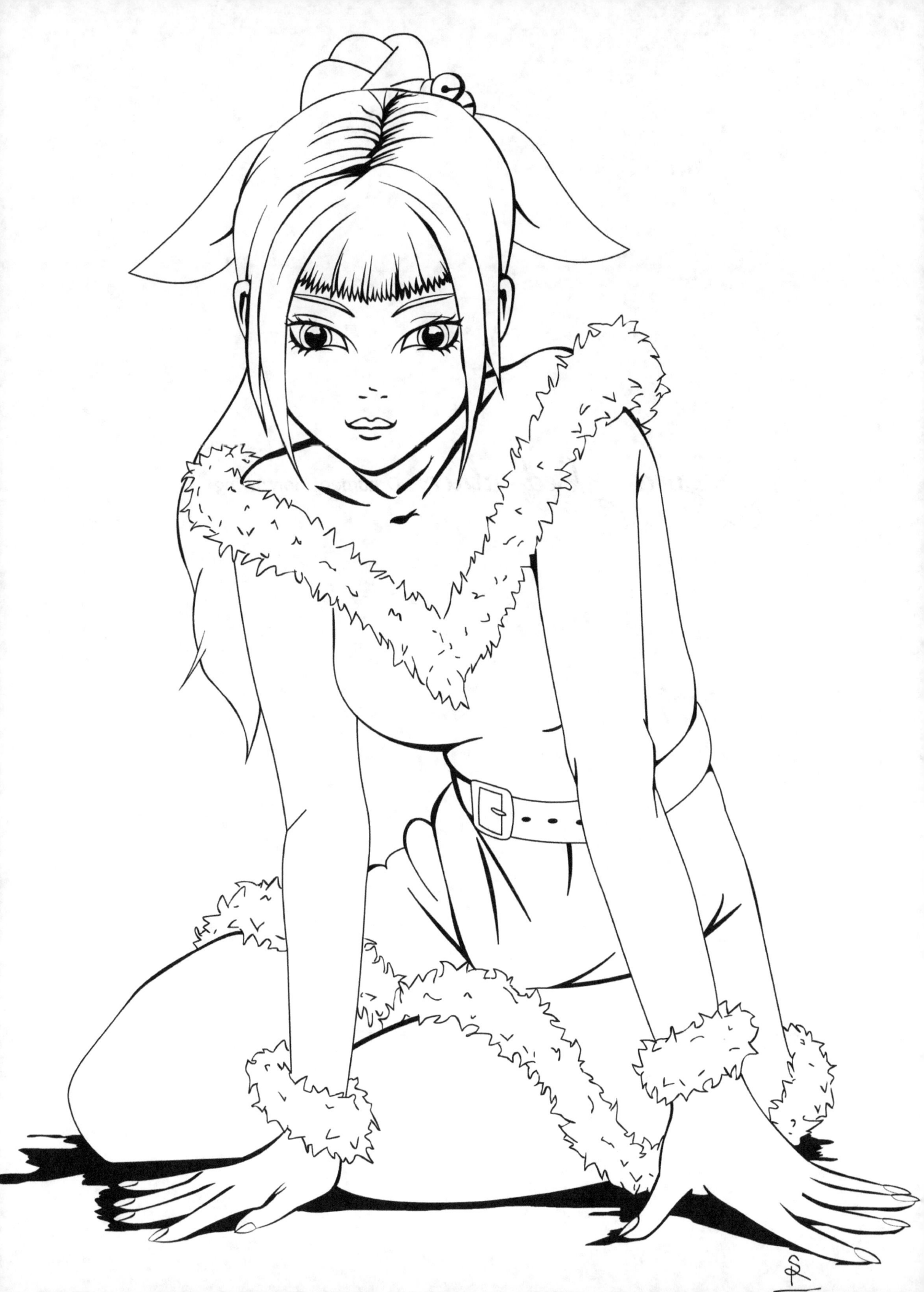

Zora Redfeather Ornament Borrowing

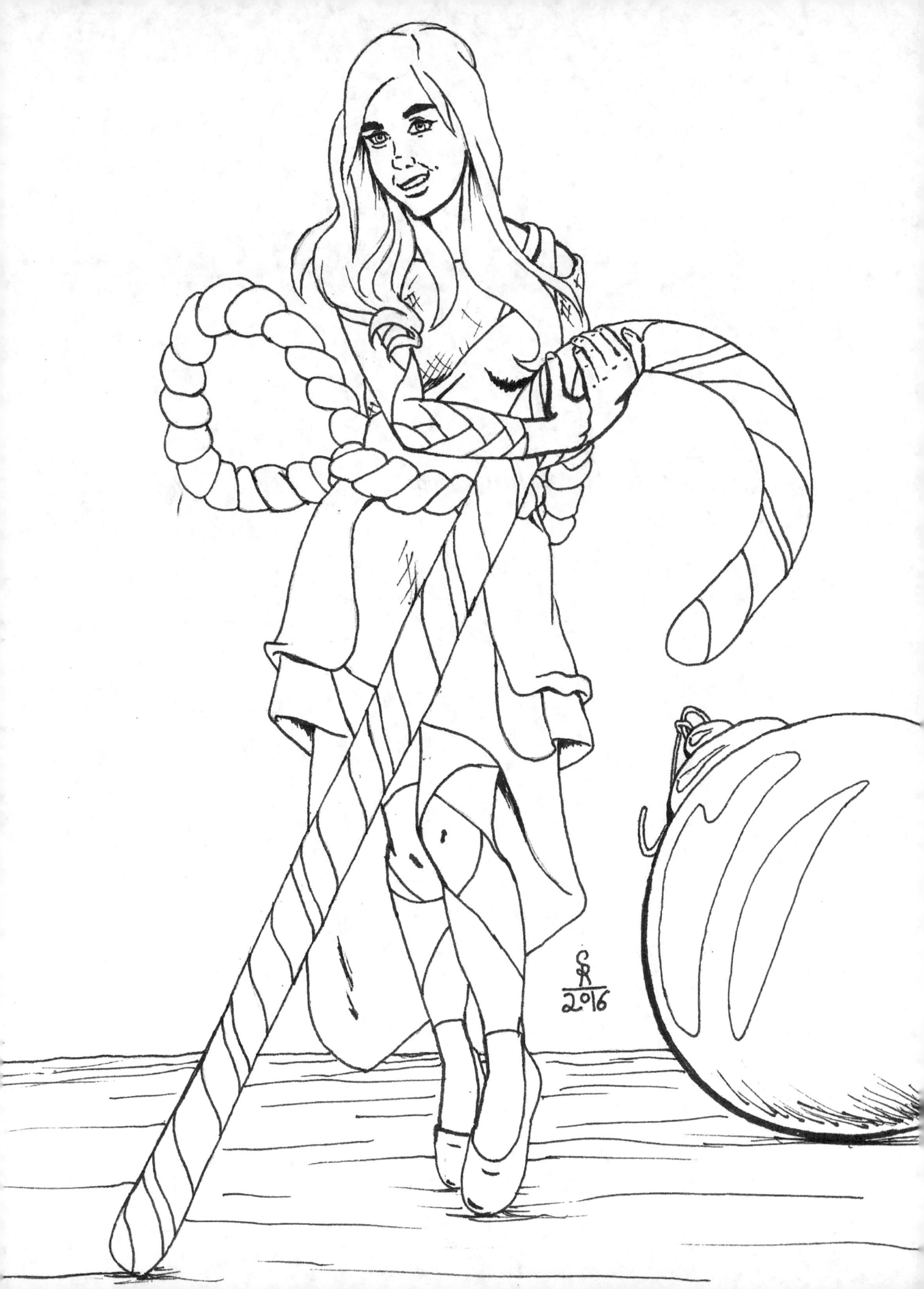

Taliah Flint Kippah

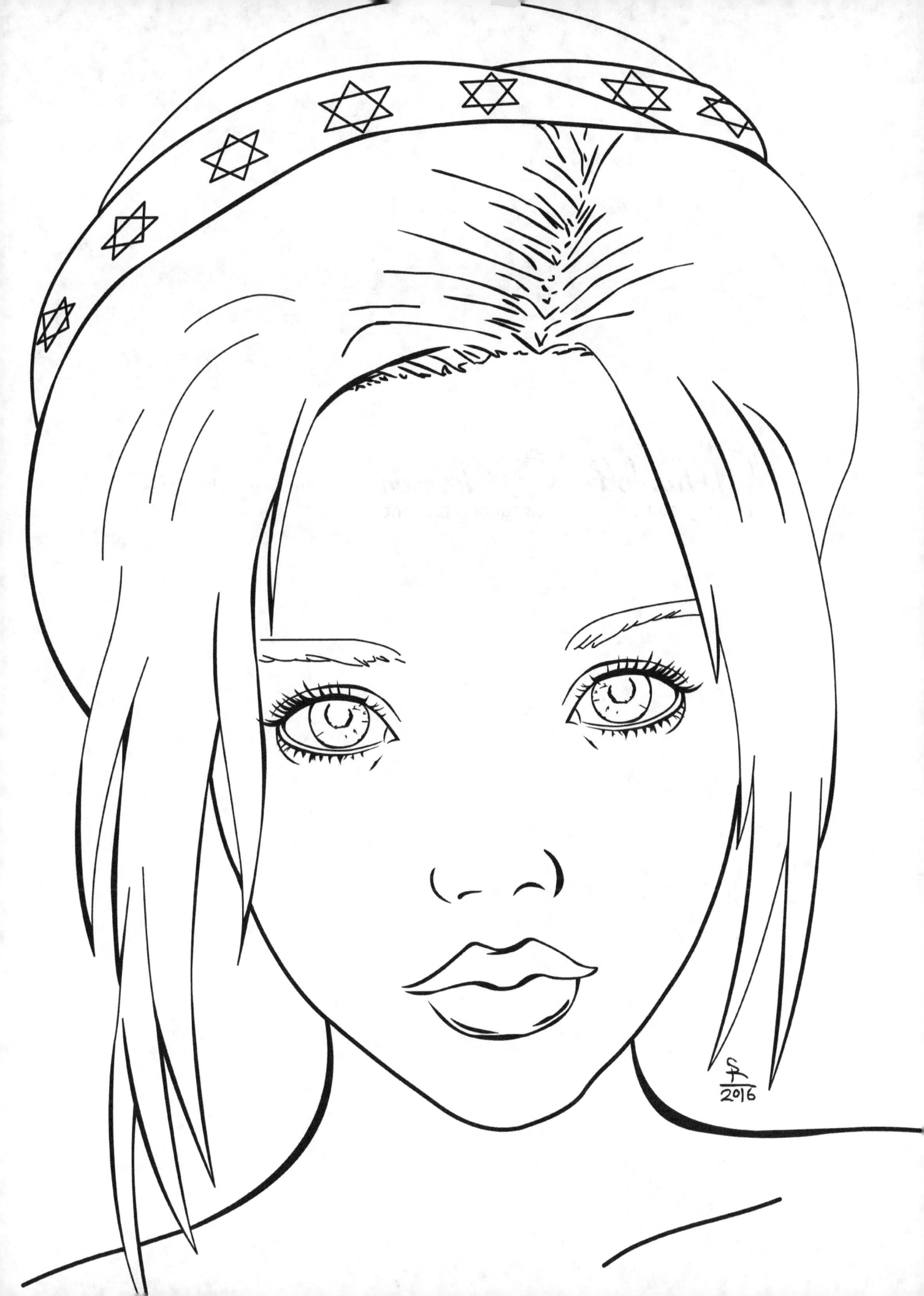

Charlotte Adamson **Present Dress** This dress is designed to look like a wrapped present.

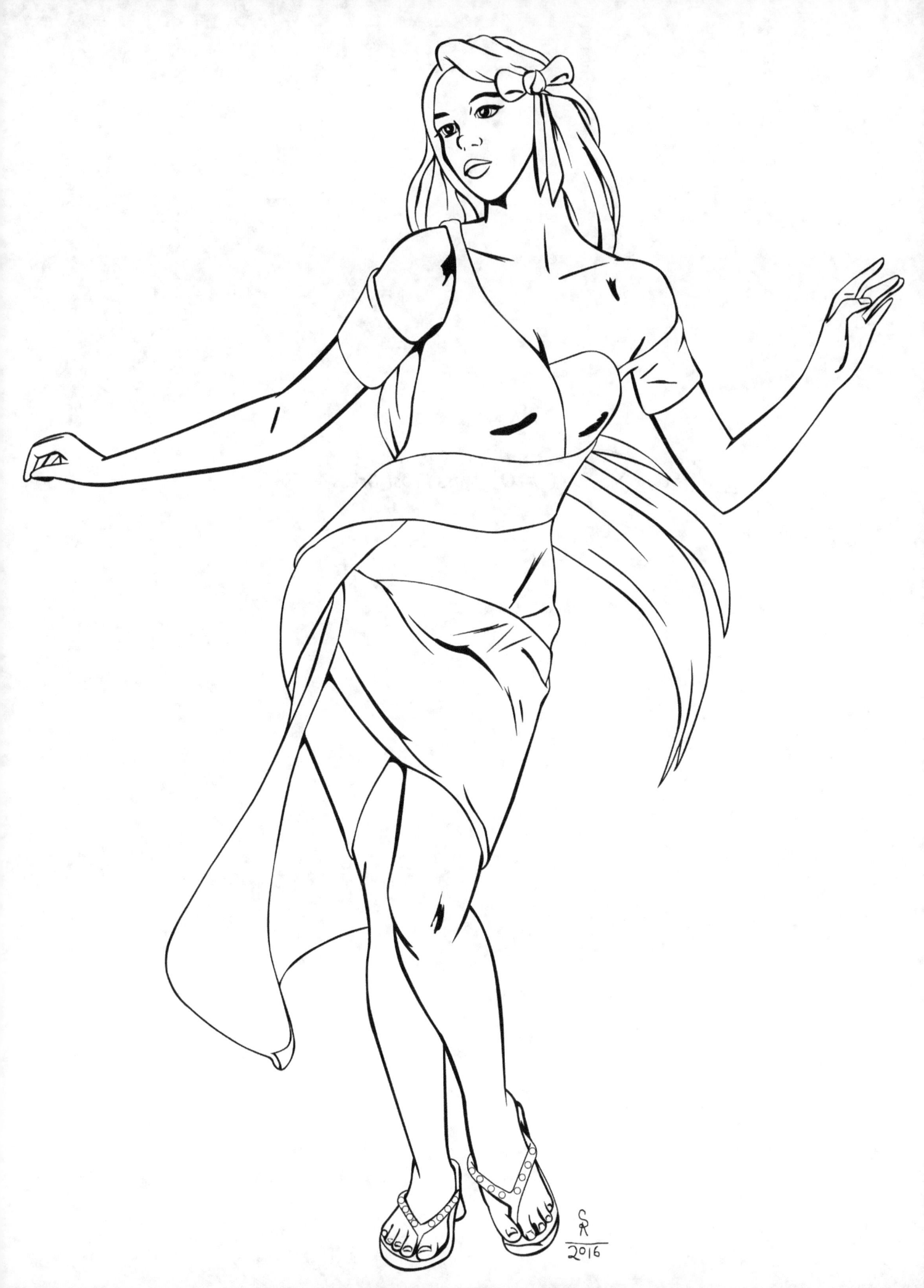

Aisa Sno Miss Frost Dress

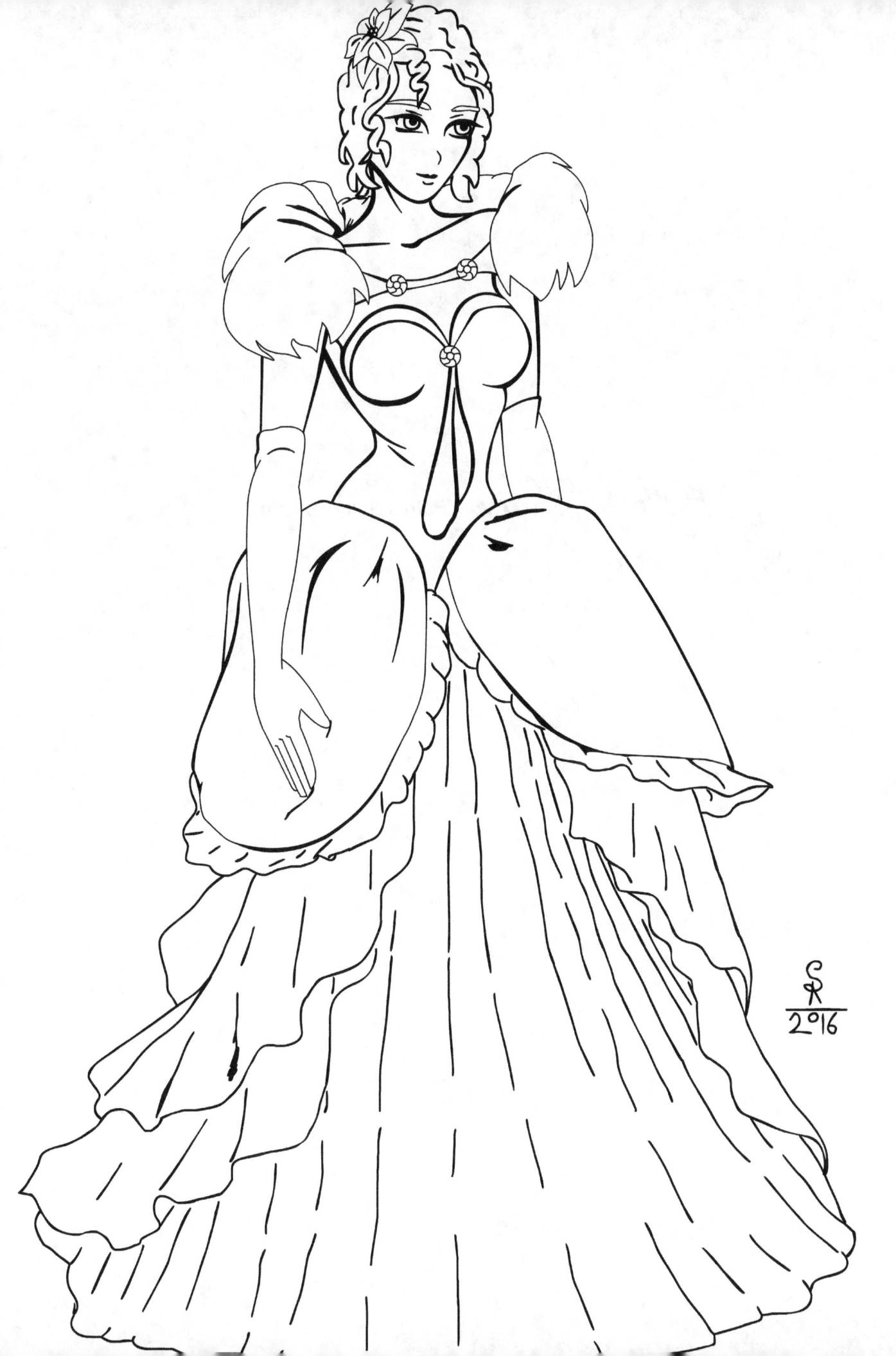

Halli's Chaise Halli's Holly Hairpin

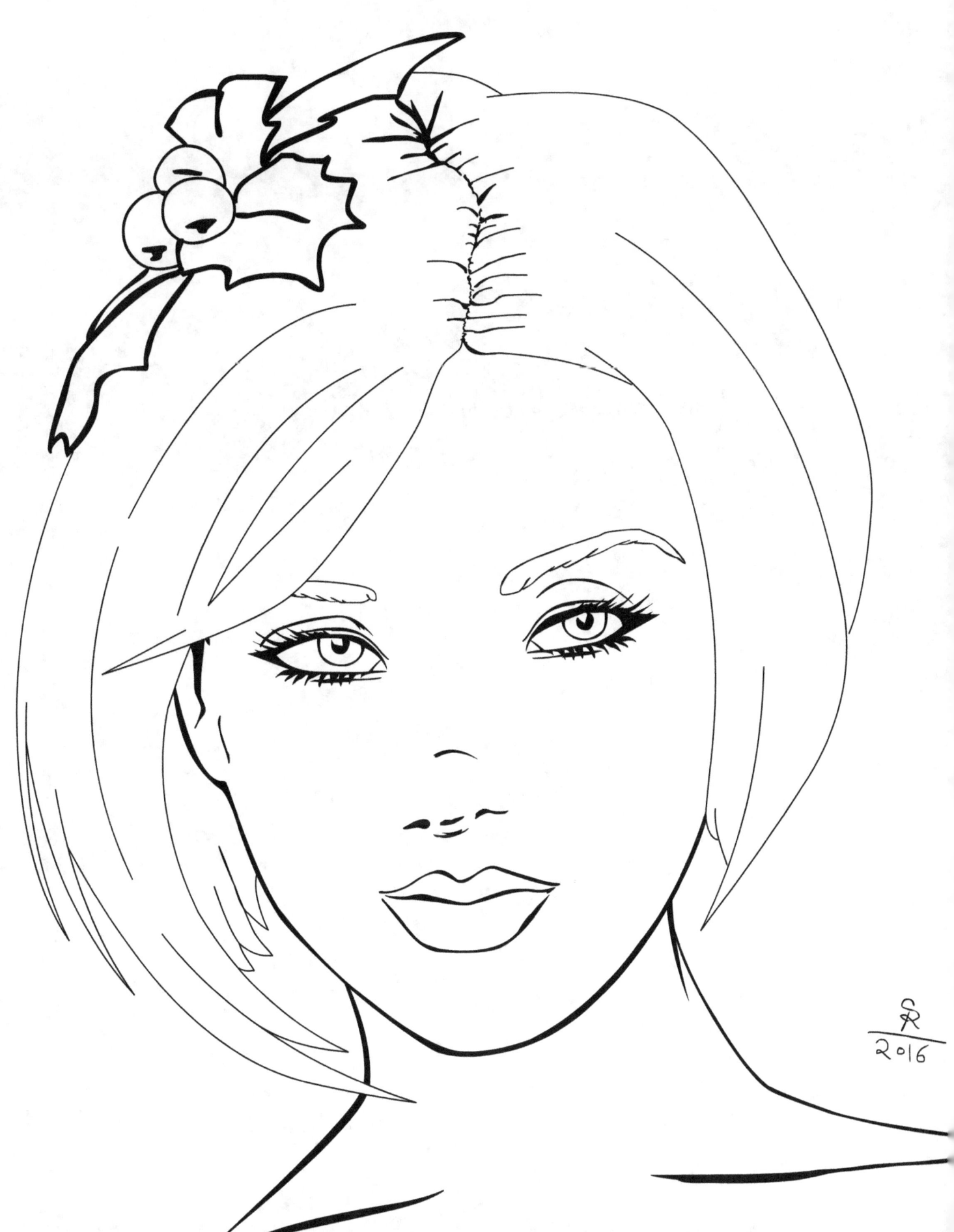

Rosemary Magen David Dress

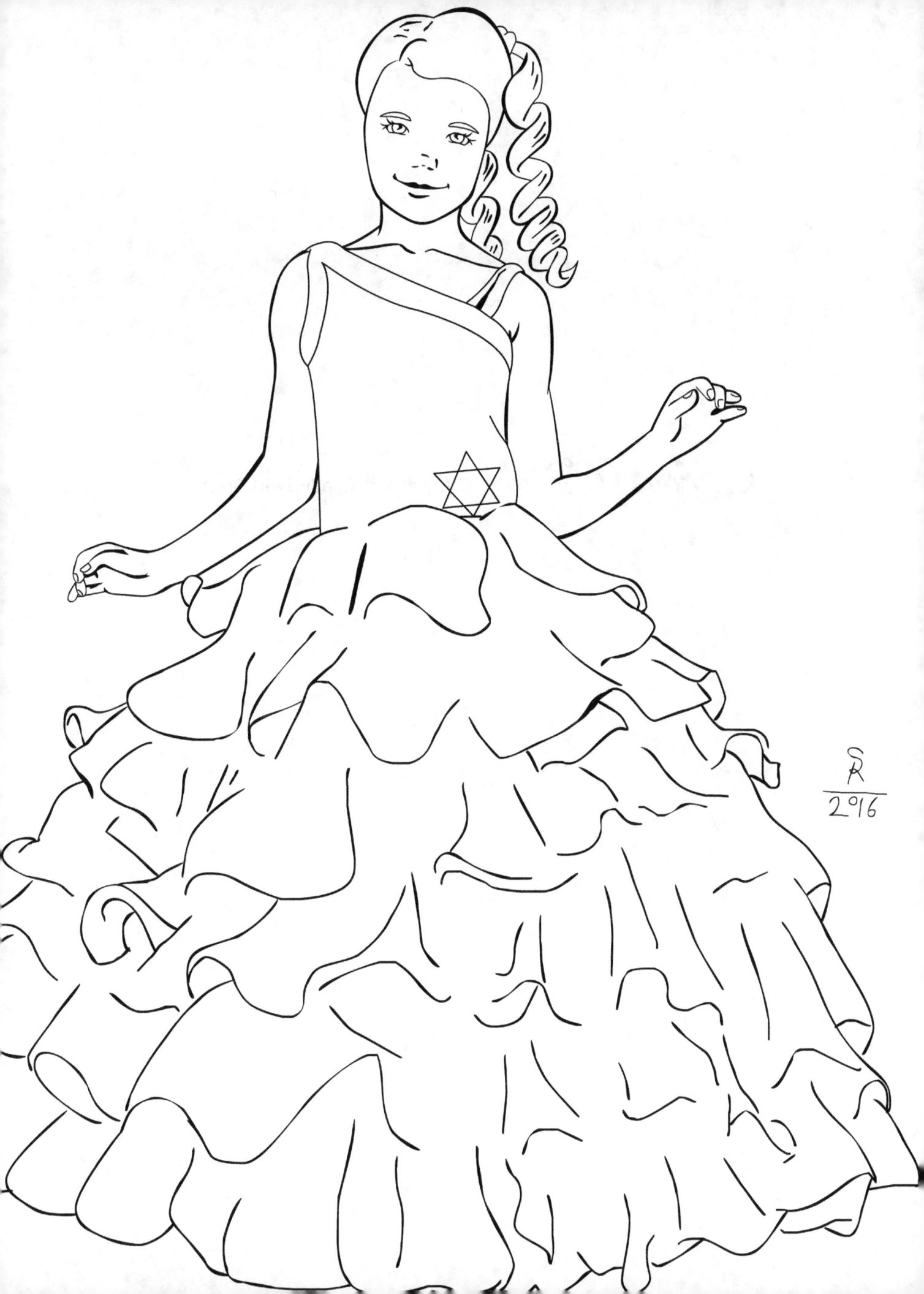

Ada Bear Gift-Bearer. Candy Swirl Dress.

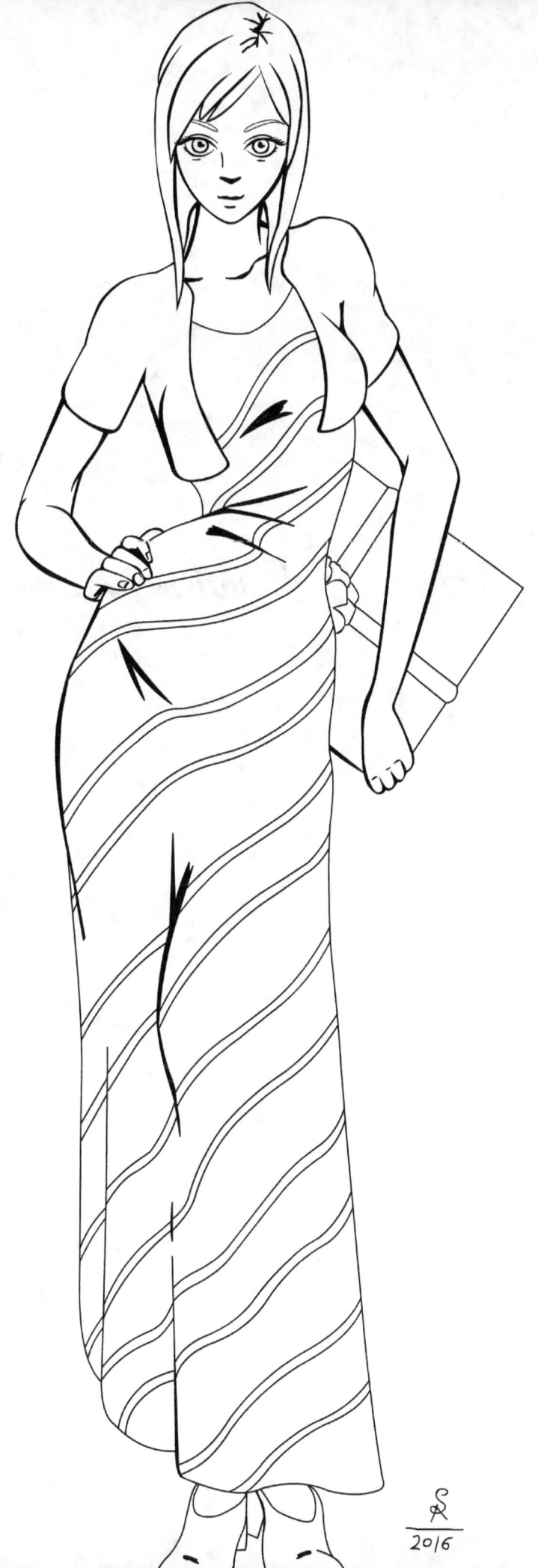

Heidi Thunderwick *Winter Maiden Dress*

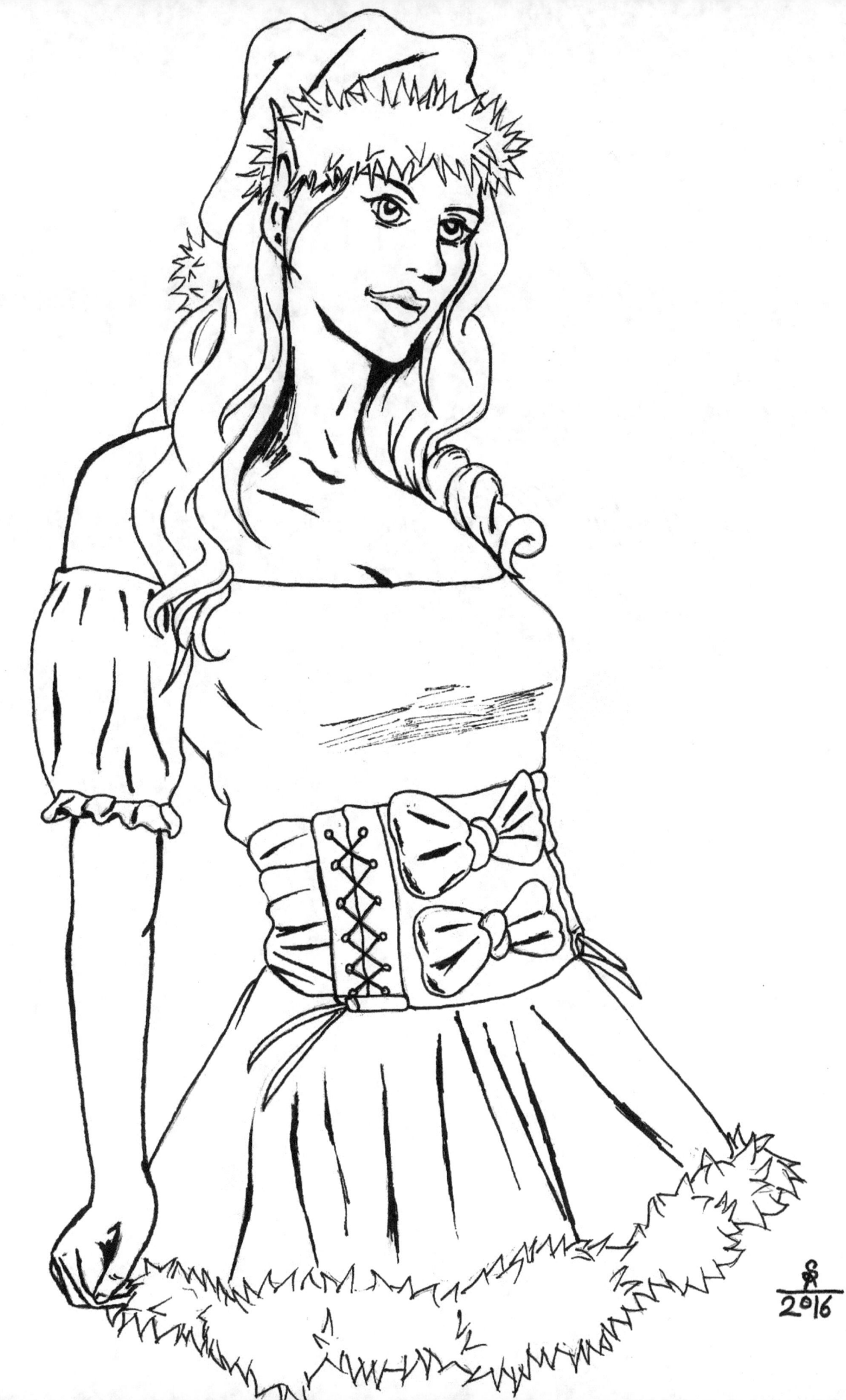

Robin Fox Holy Star Dress

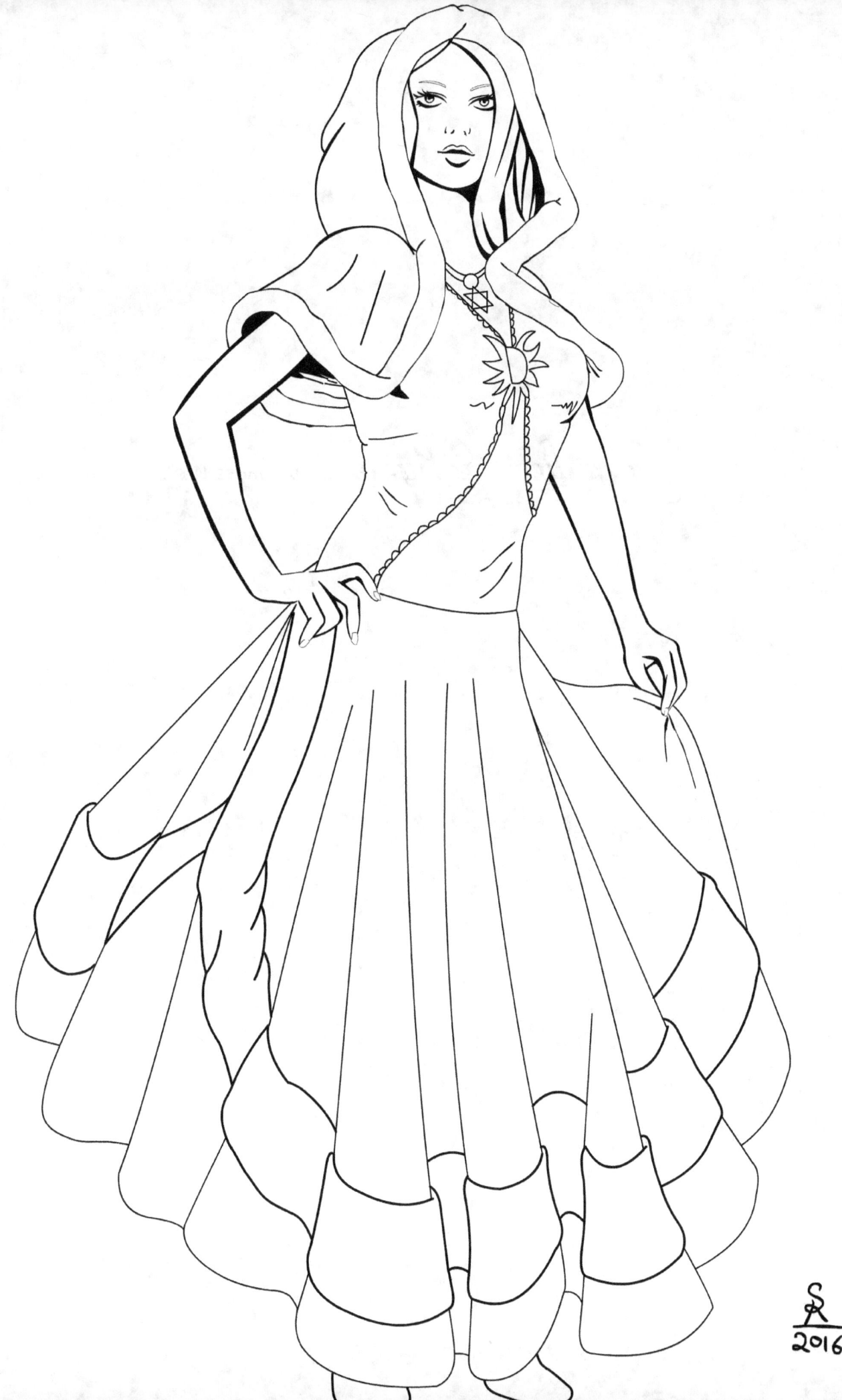

Kandice Kaine Noble Muse Dress

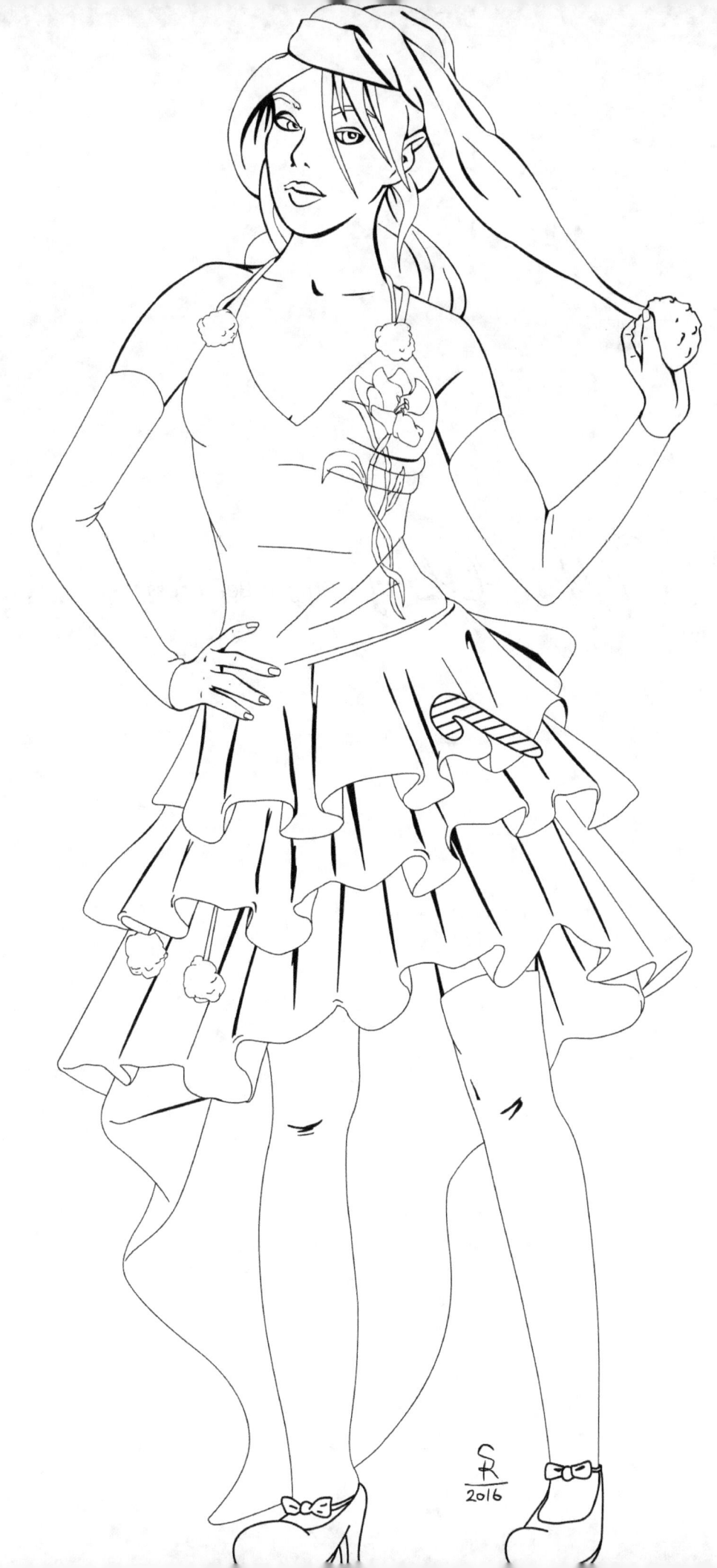

Mai Ling Dragon-Bell Dress

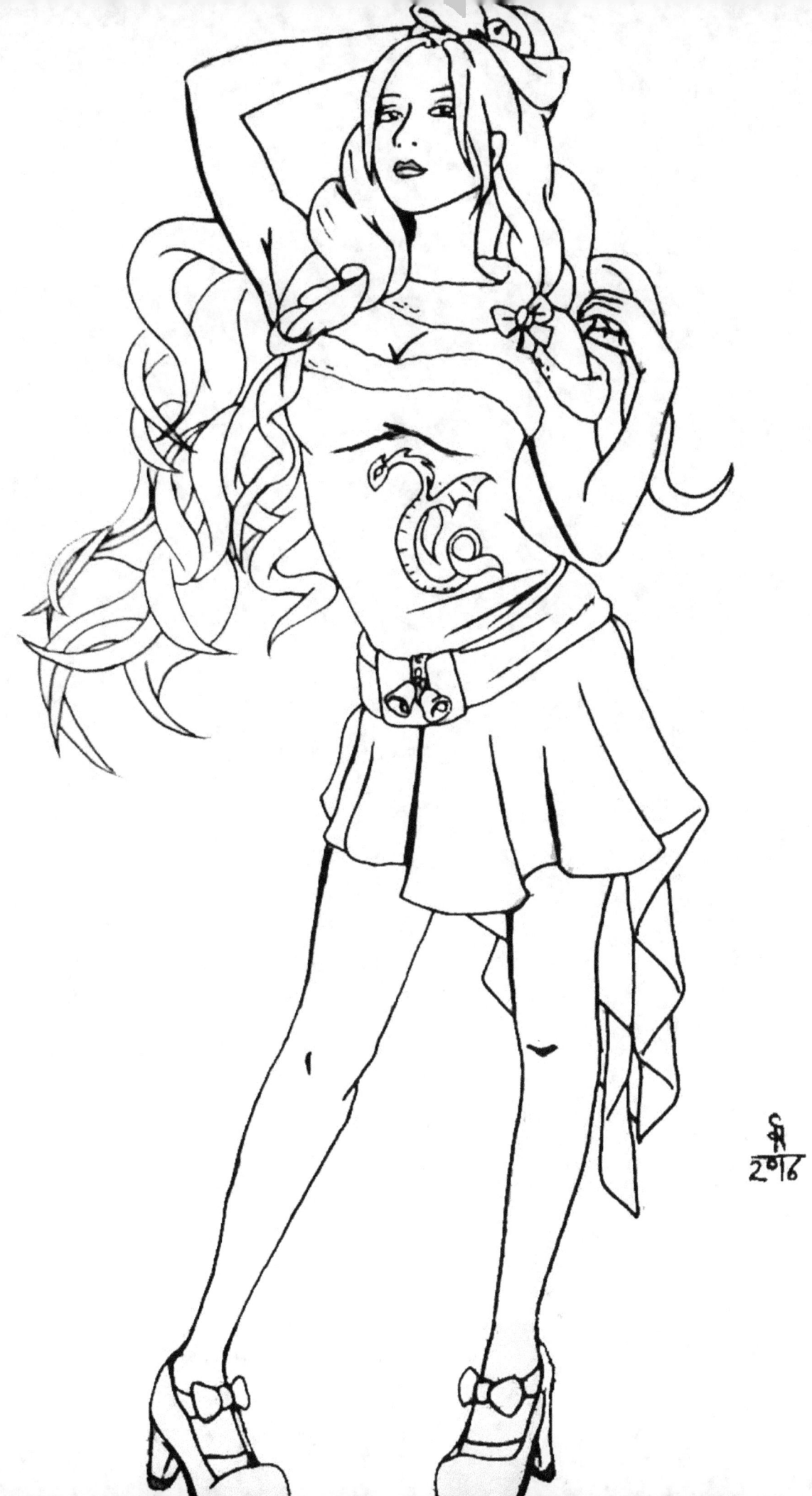

Horizontal Formats

Janaya Snowquiver Opening Presents

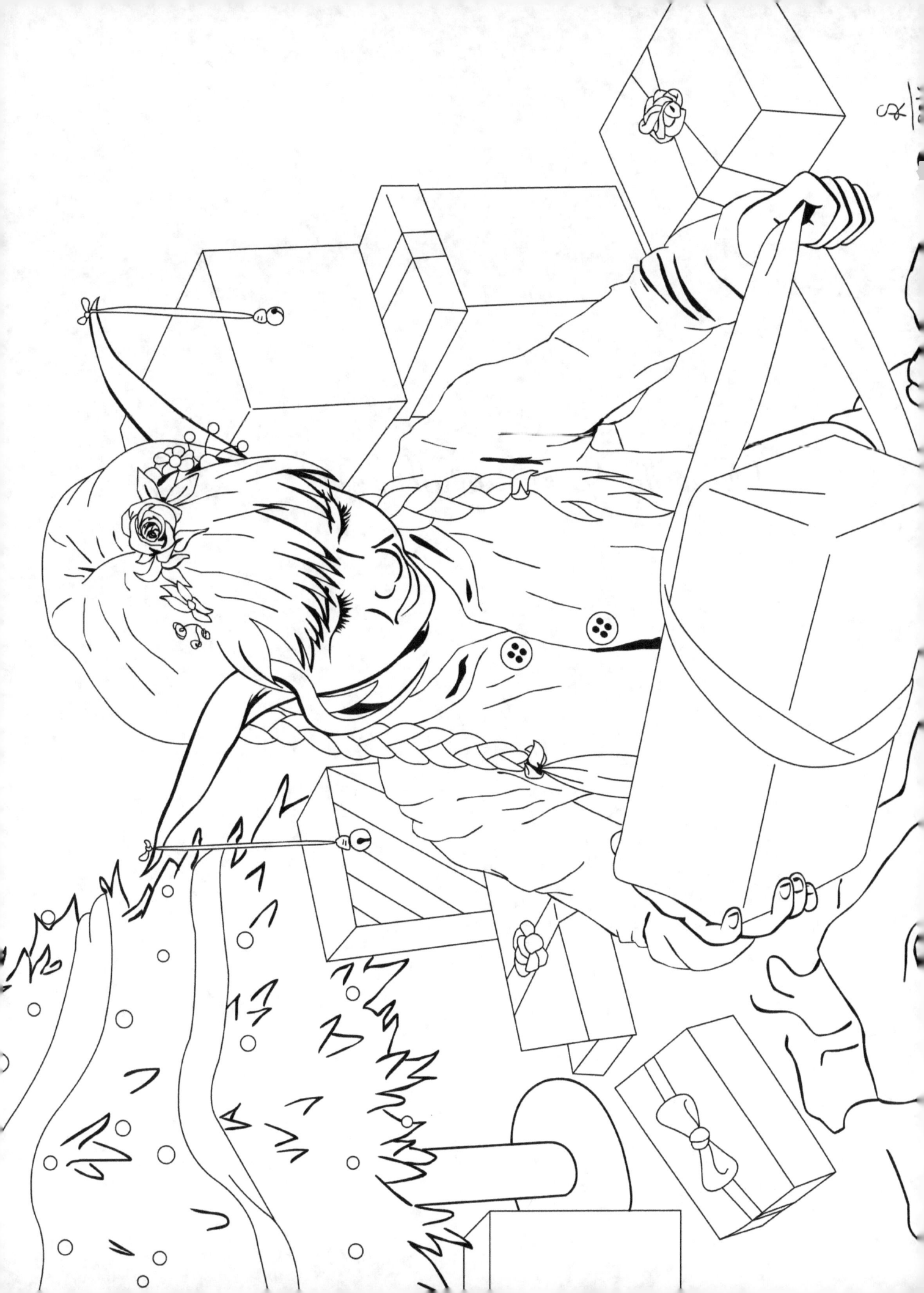

Isabella Starfall Dreidel

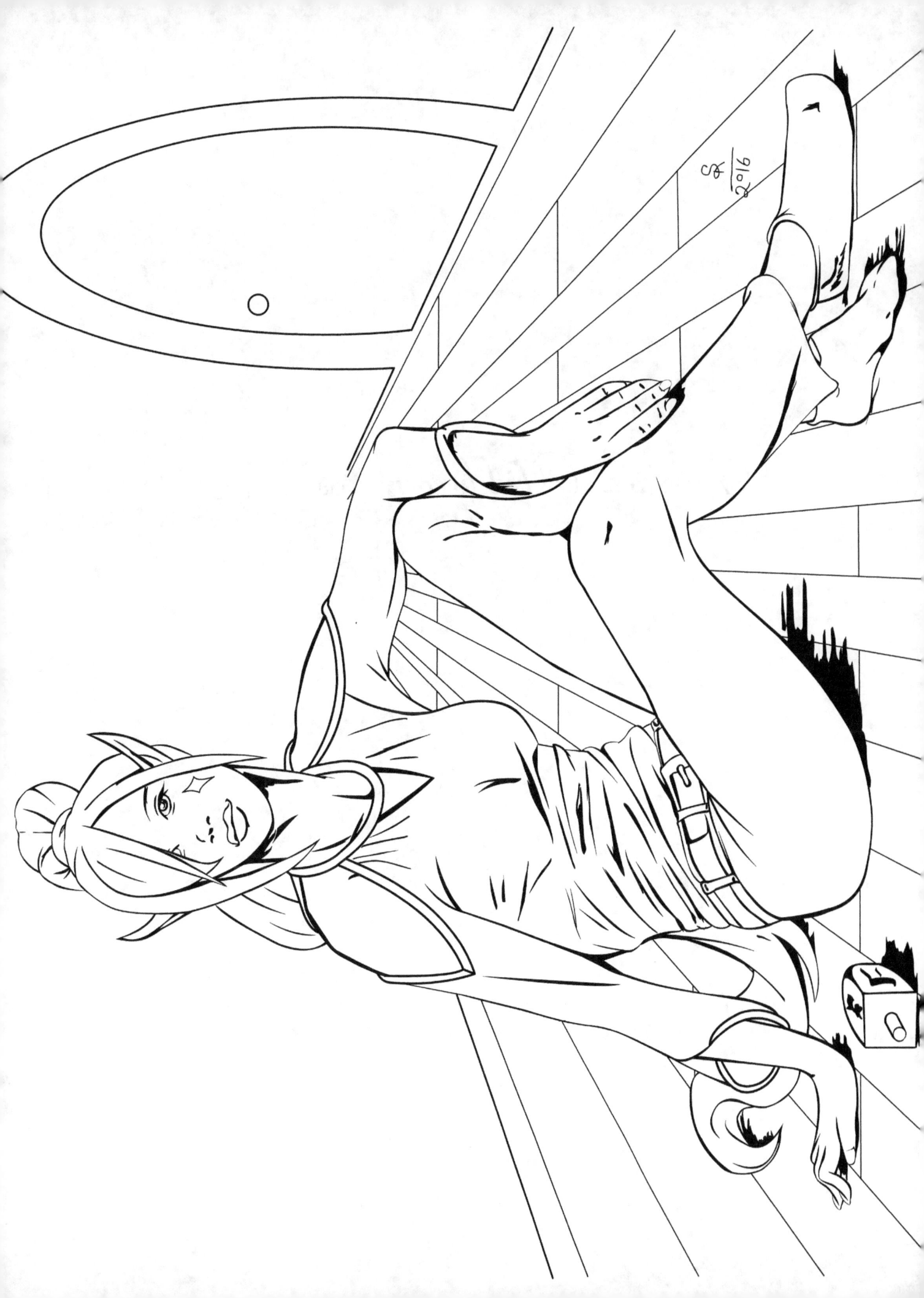

Amara Tidekeeper Holiday Shopping

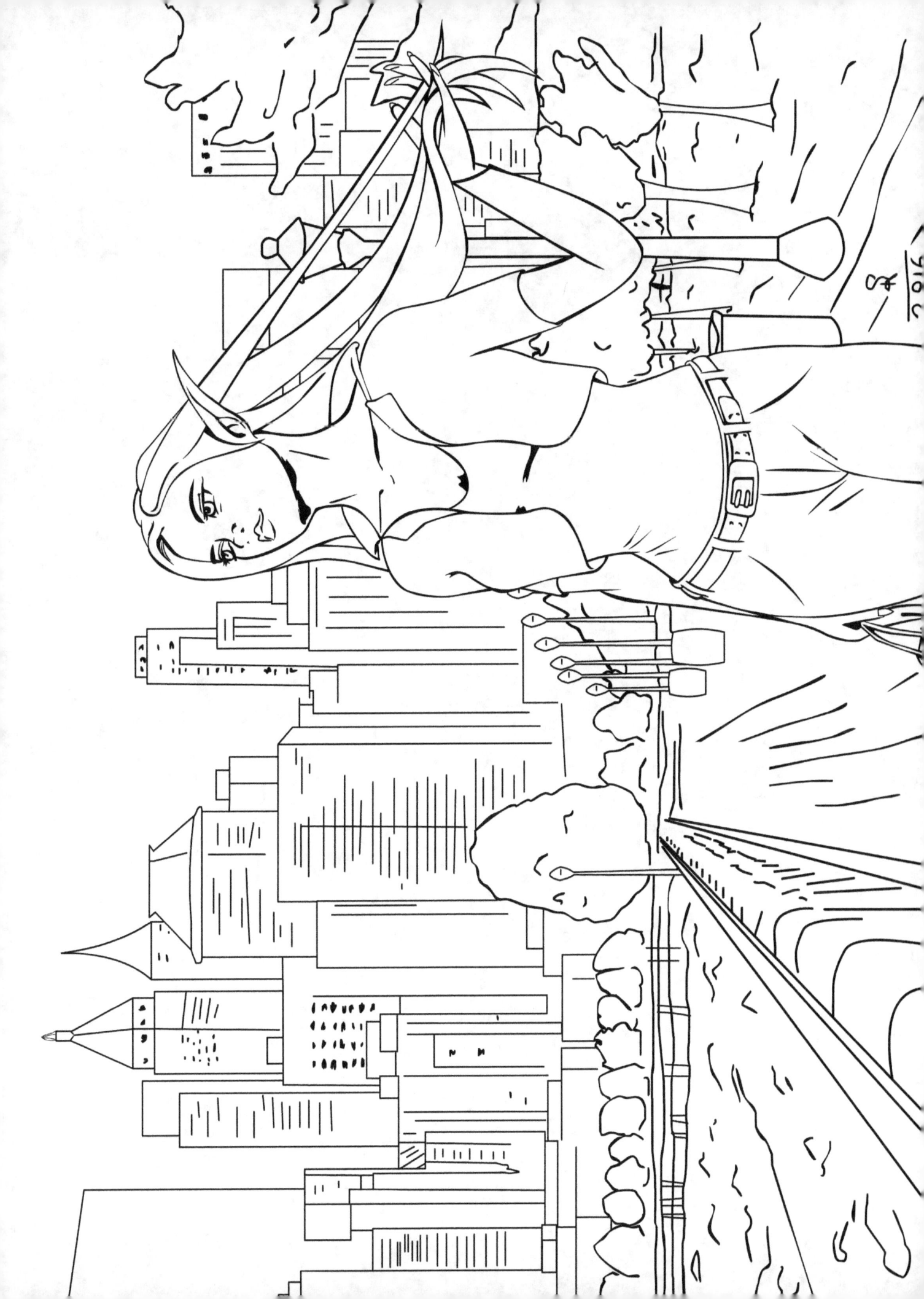

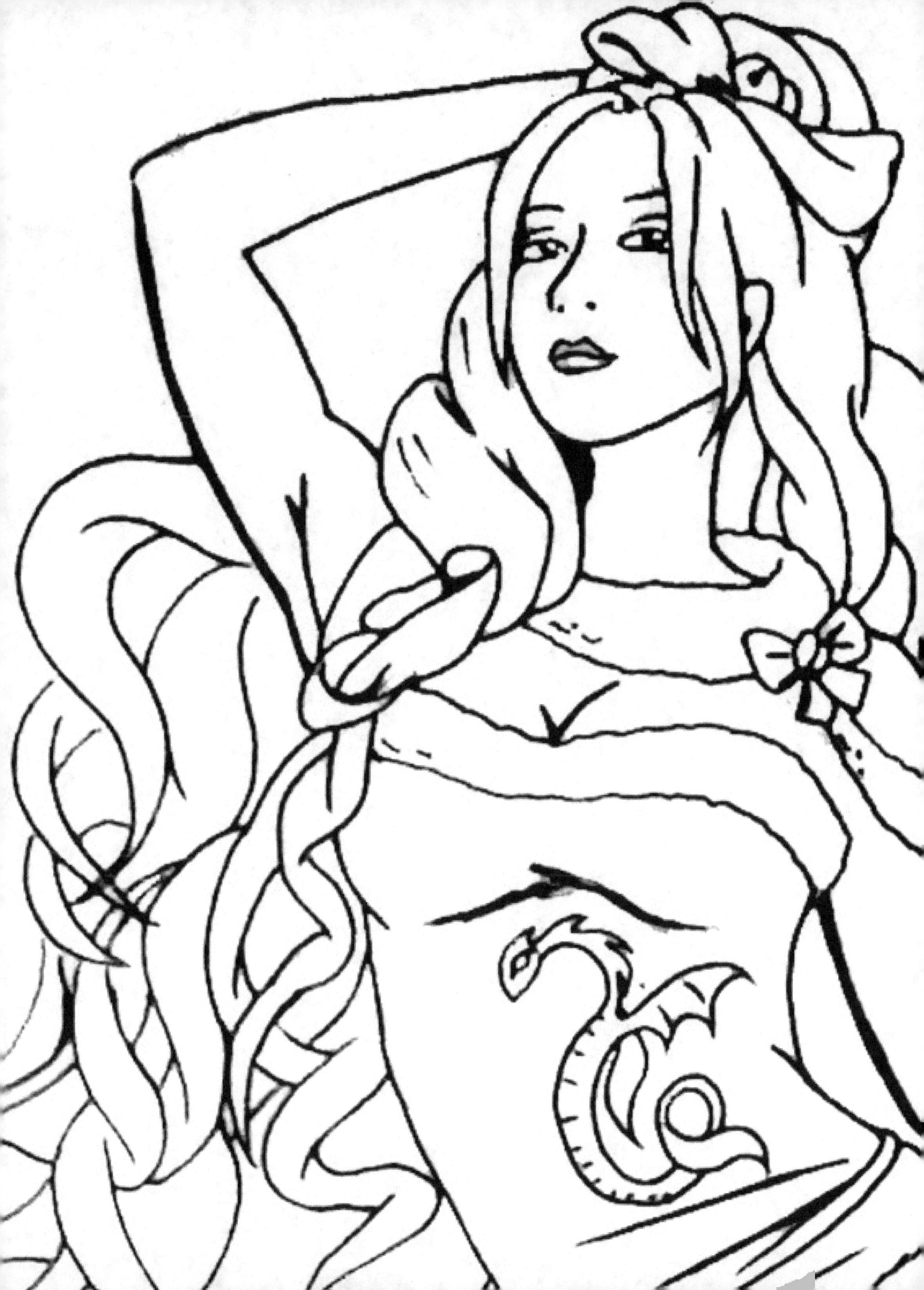

Thank you!
Look forward to my next book; Gothic Beauties,
coming Fall 2017

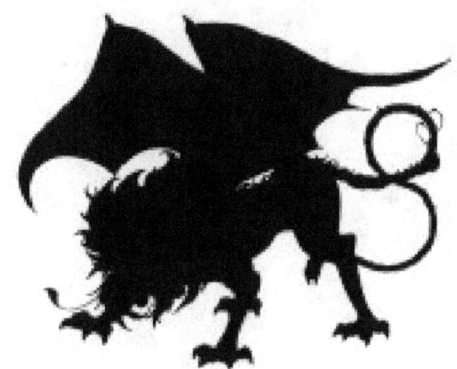

www.cheetahryu.weebly.com

www.ingramcontent.com/pod-product-compliance
Lightning Source LLC
Chambersburg PA
CBHW081302180526
45170CB00007B/2535